¡TE AMO MÁS! IS SPANISH FOR I LOVE YOU MORE!

IN THE FOREST SO WIDE, THE CAPYBARA SAYS WITH PRIDE, 'I LOVE YOU!' '¡TE AMO MÁS!' REPLIES THE TAPIR, UNDER THE SKY SO BLUE.

AT THE RIVER'S BEND, THE AXOLOTL GRINS, 'I LOVE YOU!' FROM THE BANK, THE COATI SHOUTS BACK, '¡TE AMO MÁS!

BENEATH THE OLD OAK TREE, THE PANGOLIN SAYS SHYLY, 'I LOVE YOU!' '¡TE AMO MÁS!' CHIRPS THE QUOKKA, QUITE SPRIGHTLY.

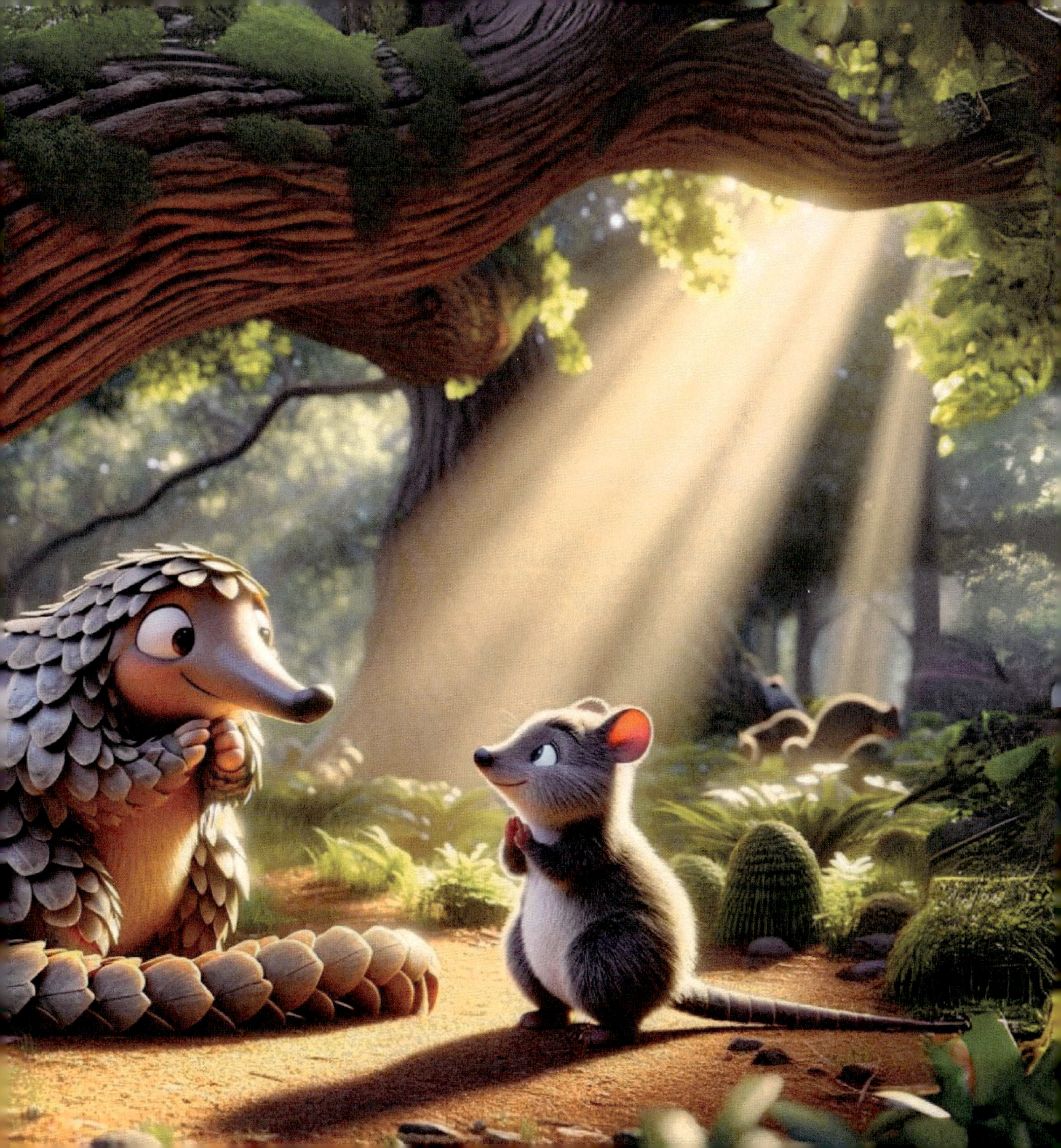

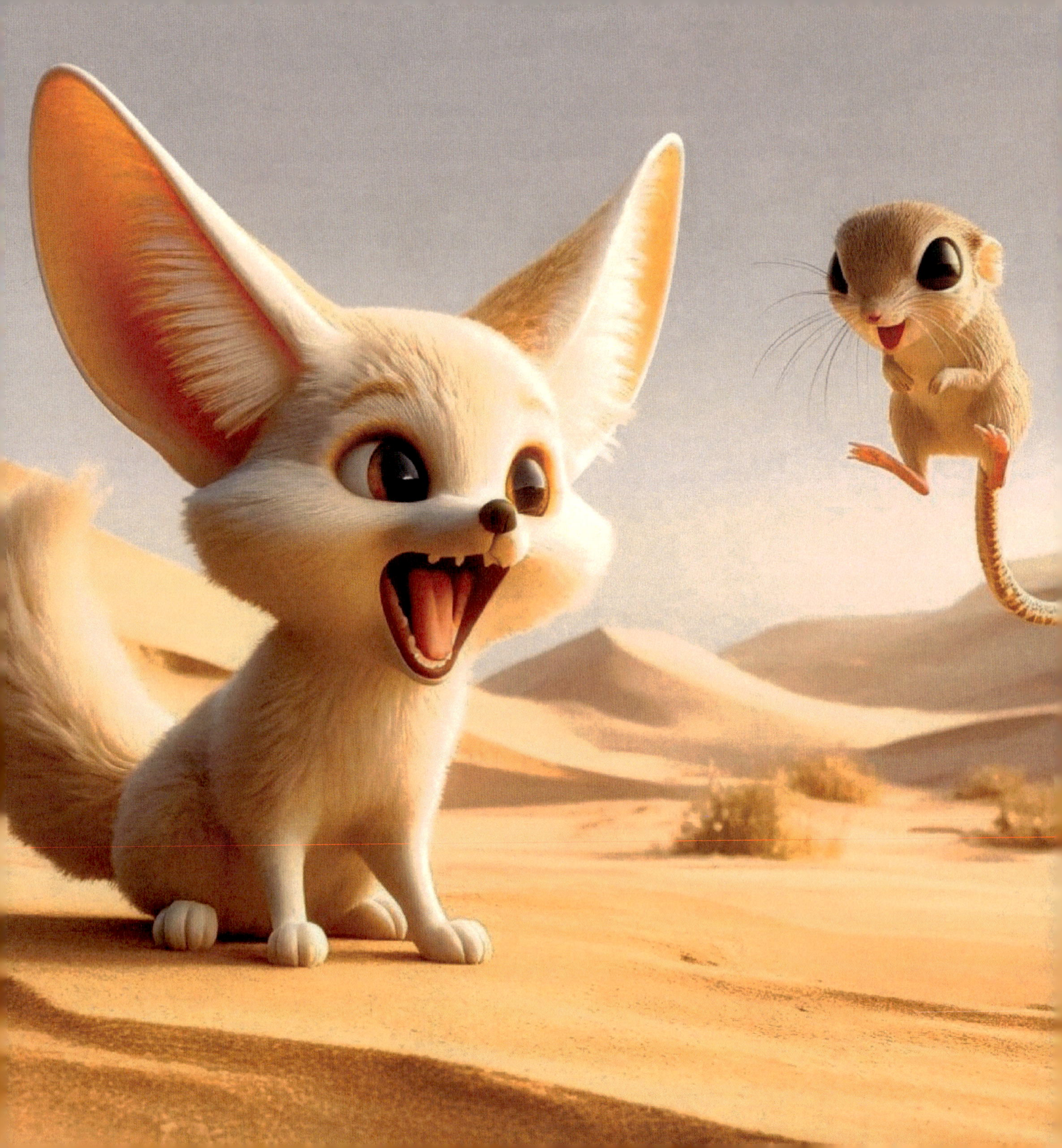

ACROSS THE SANDY SHORE, THE FENNEC FOX YELLS, 'I LOVE YOU!' '¡TE AMO MÁS!' THE JERBOA JUMPS AND TELLS.

IN THE BUSTLING REEF, THE SEAHORSE TWIRLS, 'I LOVE YOU!' '¡TE AMO MÁS!' THE COLORFUL PARROTFISH SWIRLS.

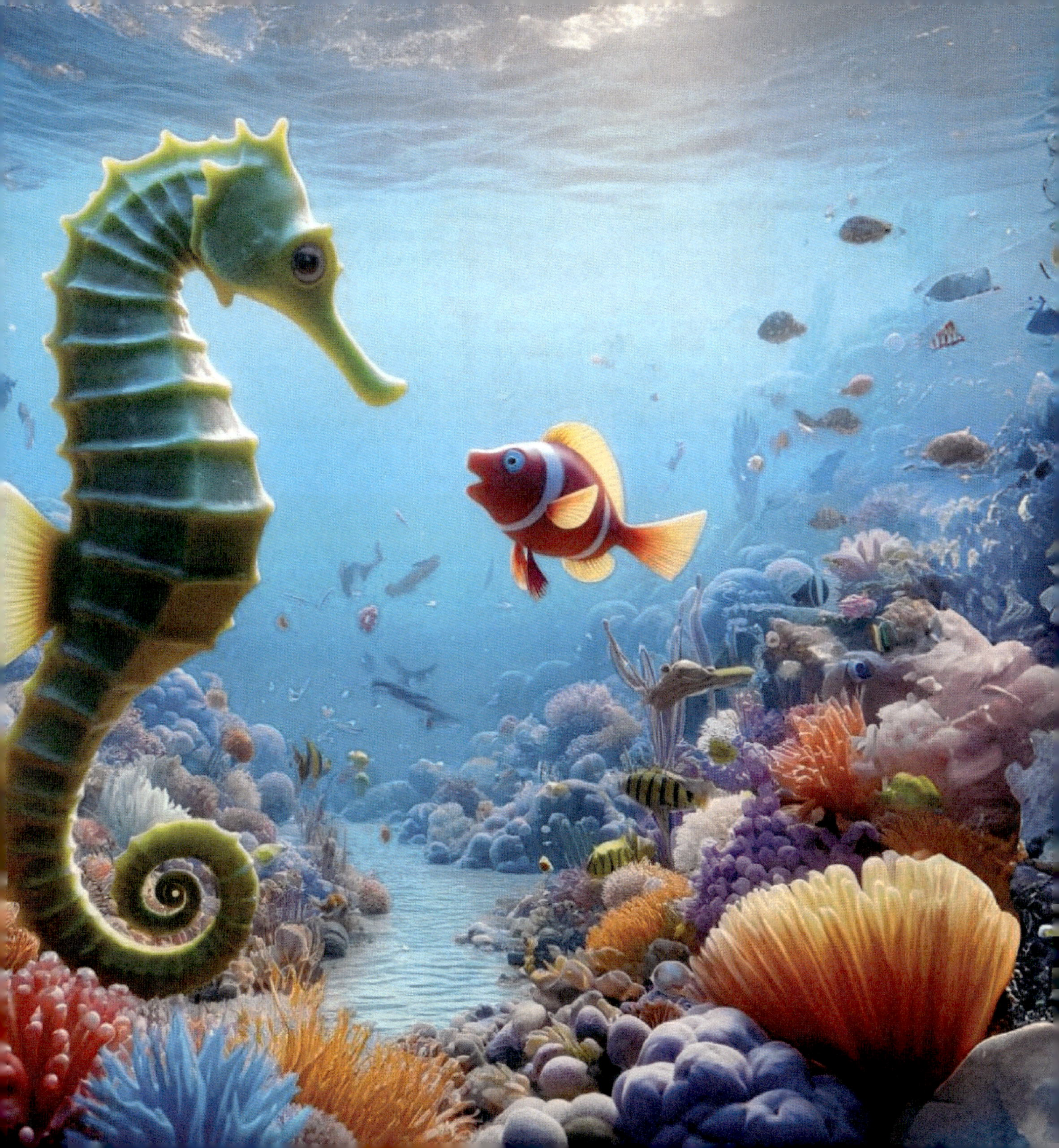

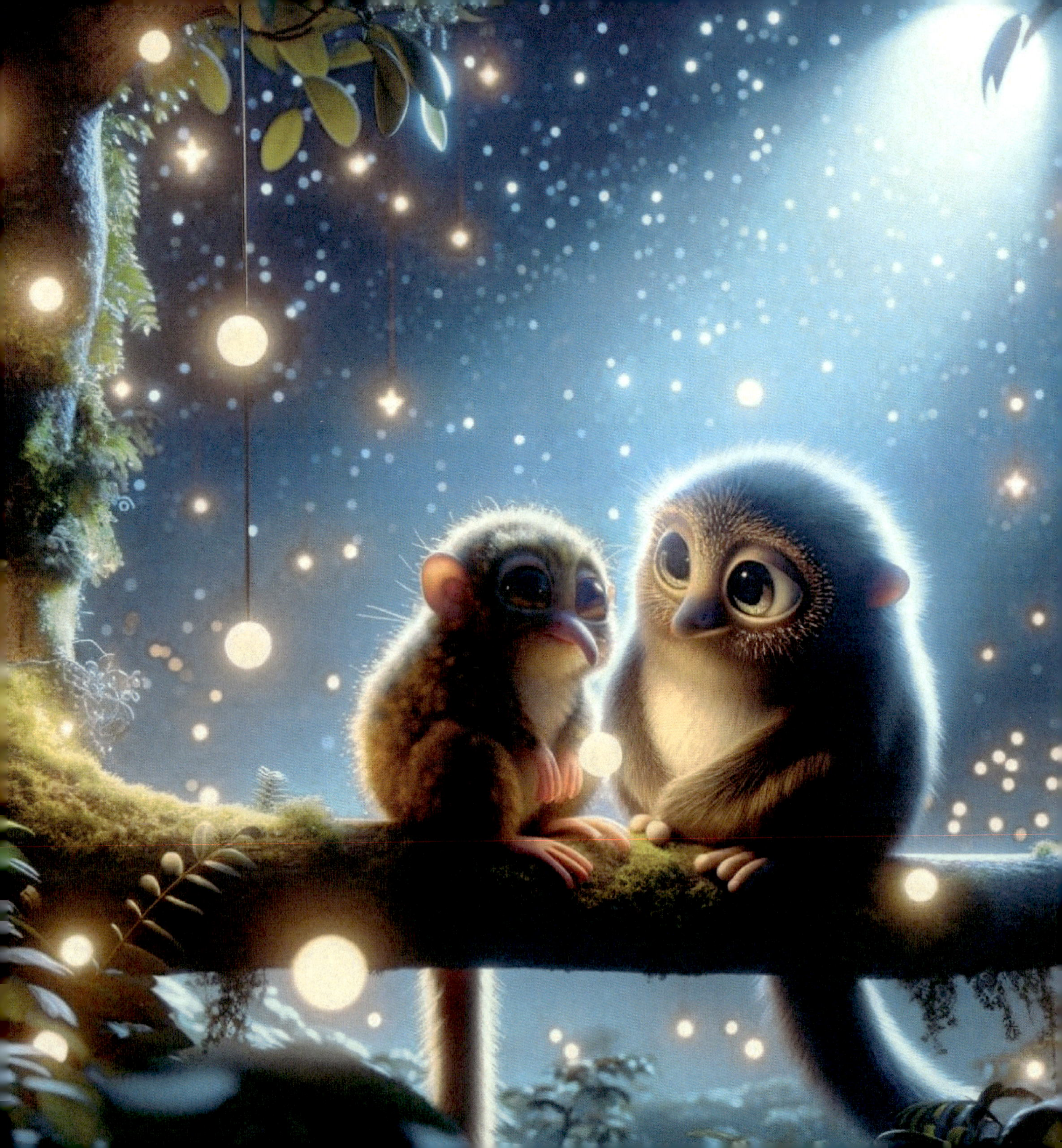

UNDER THE STARLIT SKY, THE KIWI WHISPERS SOFTLY, 'I LOVE YOU!' '¡TE AMO MÁS!' THE TARSIER REPLIES ALOFTLY.

In the cool shade of bamboo, the red panda stretches, 'I love you!' '¡Te amo más!' the slow loris fetches.

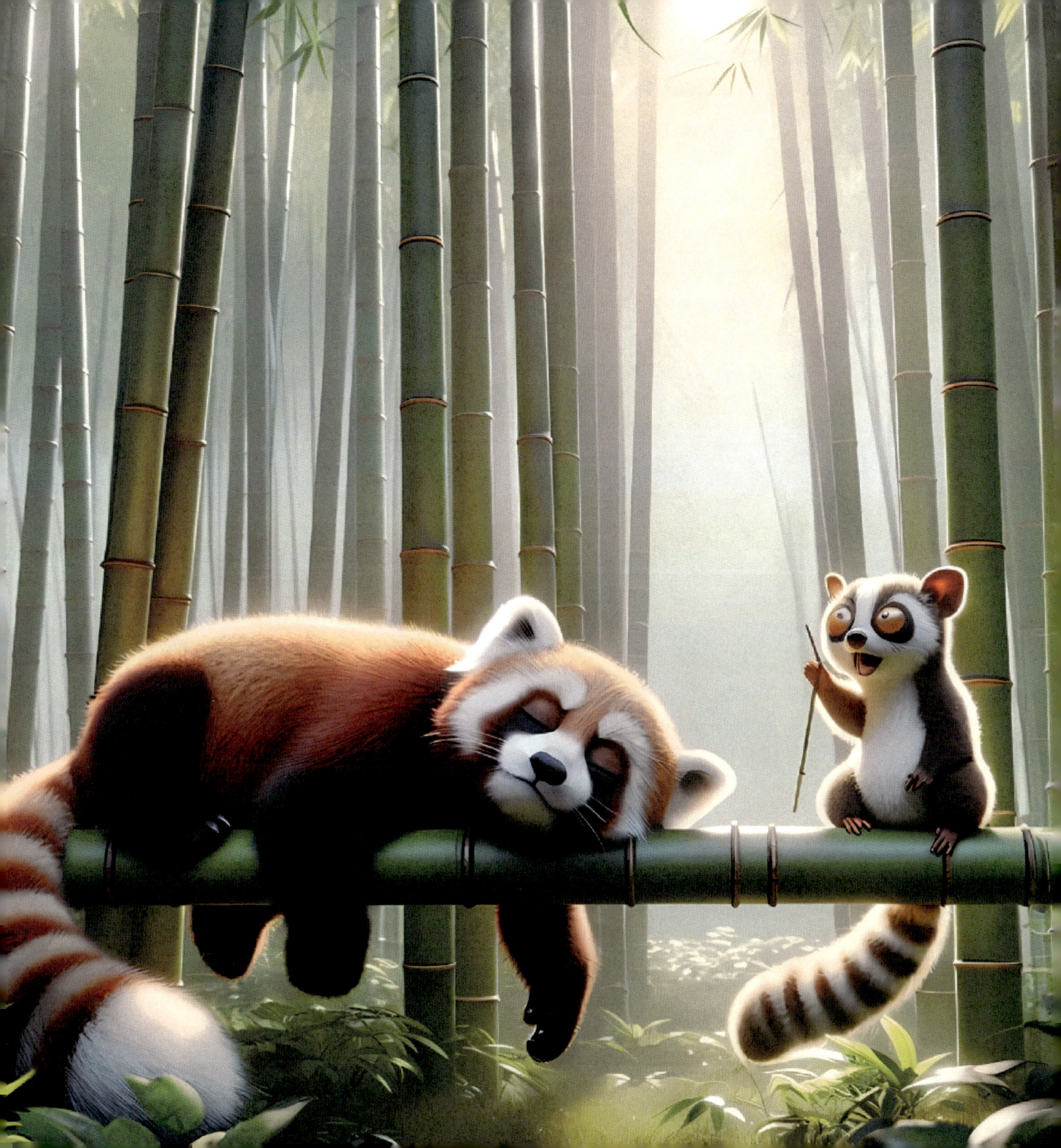

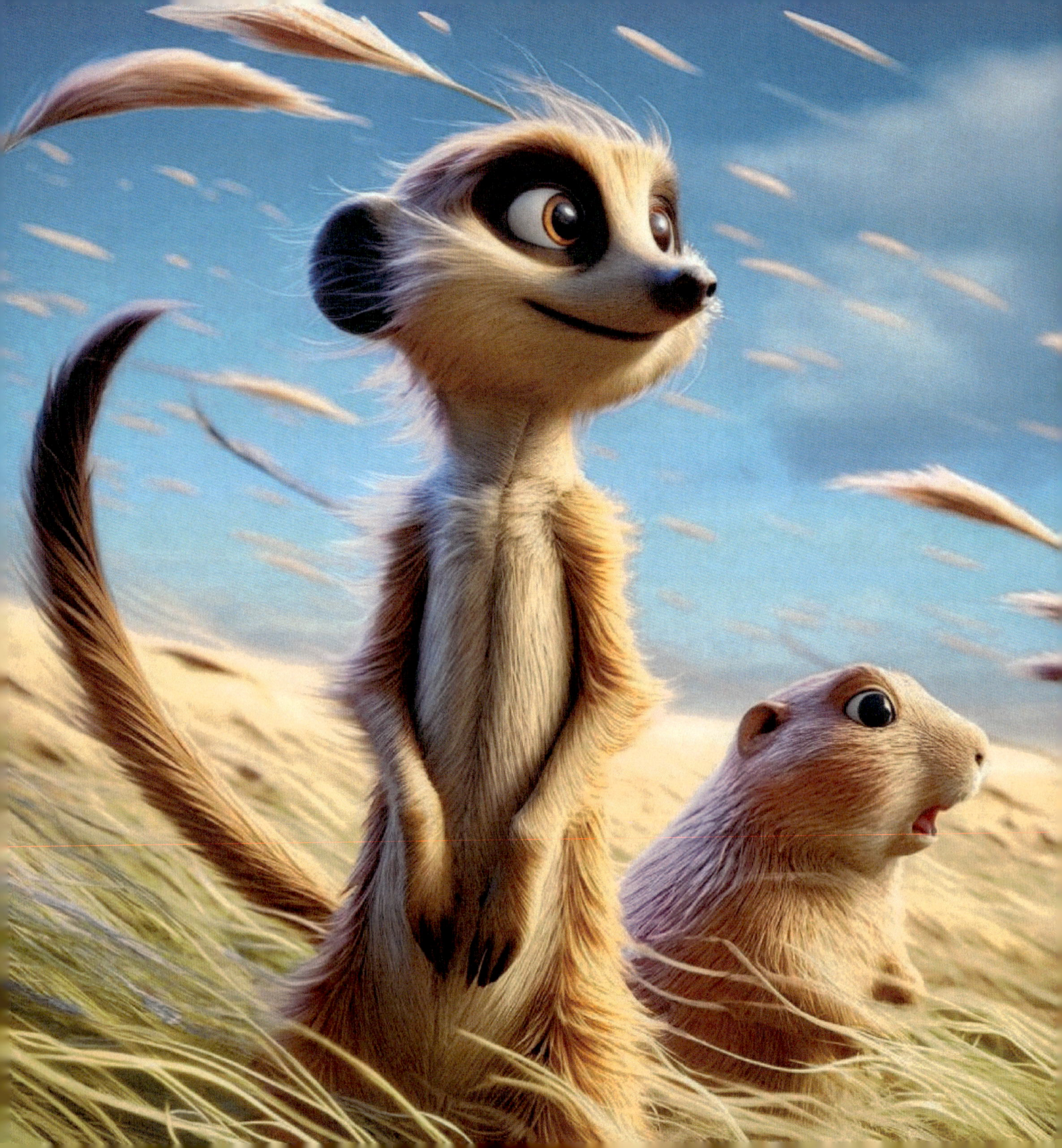

ON THE WINDY PLAINS, THE MEERKAT STANDS TALL, 'I LOVE YOU!' '¡TE AMO MÁS!' THE PRAIRIE DOG CALLS.

IN THE DENSE JUNGLE LEAVES, THE TAMARIN DECLARES, 'I LOVE YOU!' '¡TE AMO MÁS!' THE AGOUTI SHARES.

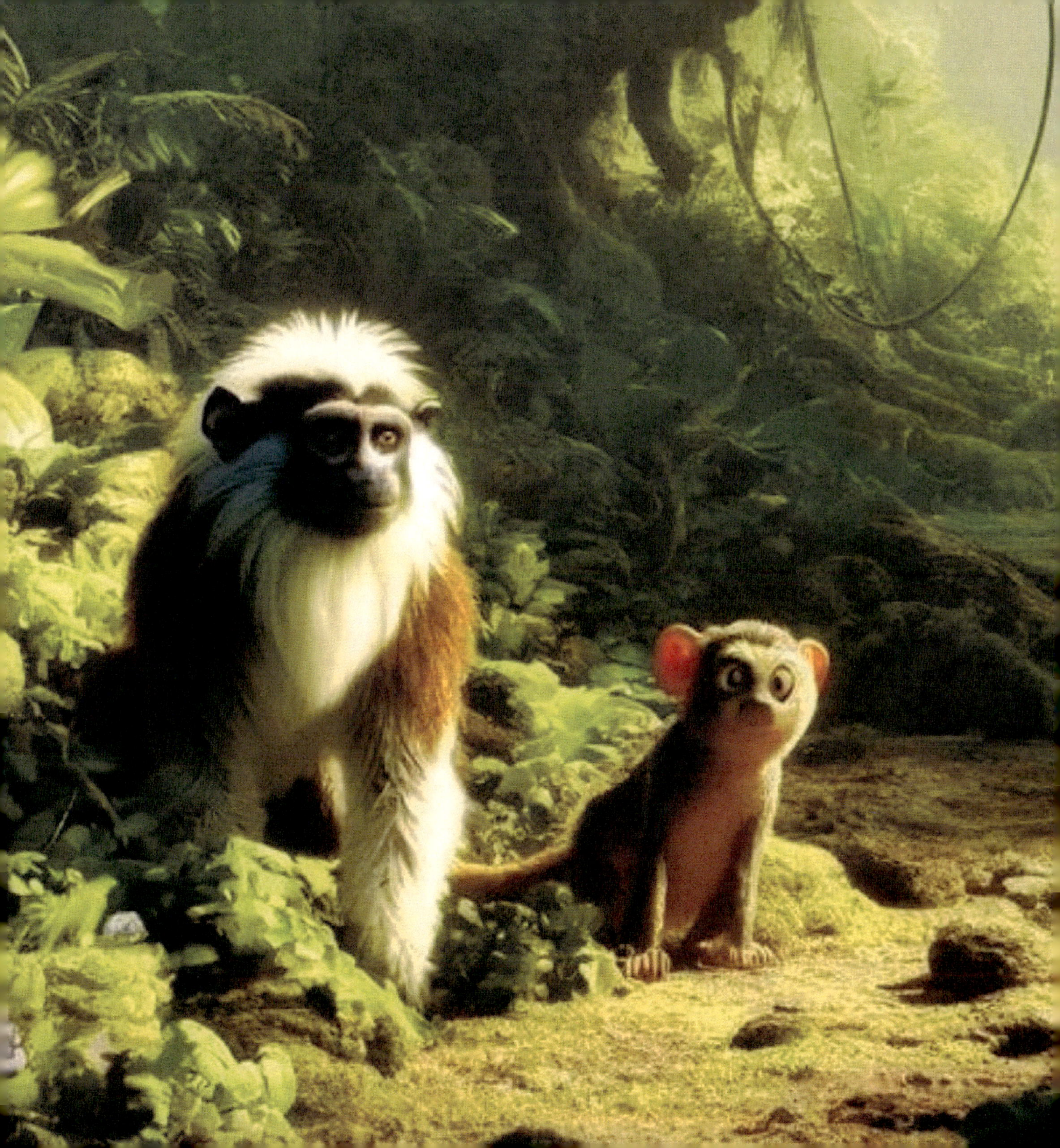

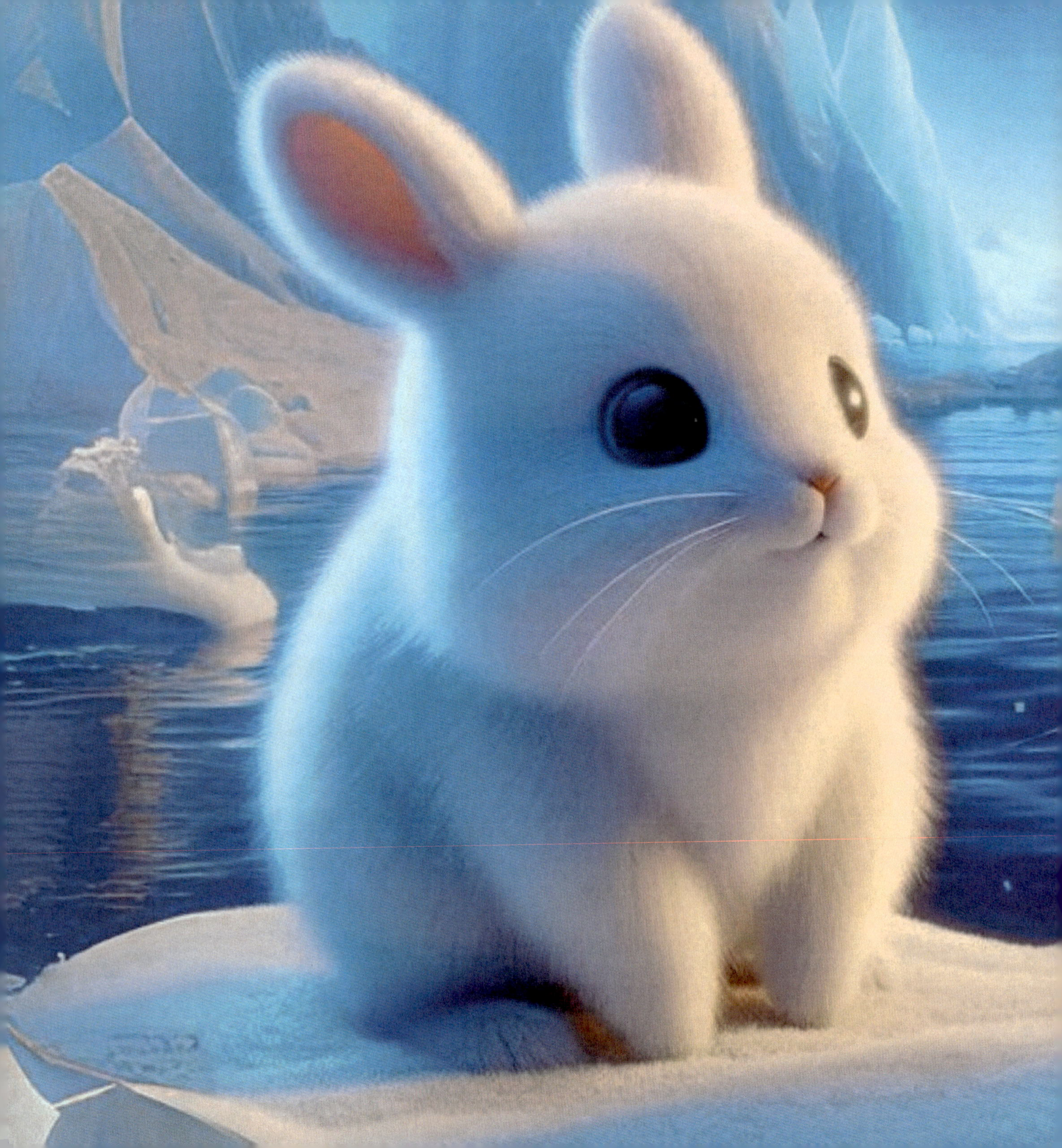

BY THE CHILLY ICEBERG, THE PIKA SQUEAKS, 'I LOVE YOU!' '¡TE AMO MÁS!' THE ARCTIC HARE SPEAKS.

IN THE TALL GRASS AT DAWN, THE SUGAR GLIDER SOARS, 'I LOVE YOU!' '¡TE AMO MÁS!' THE BUSH BABY IMPLORES.

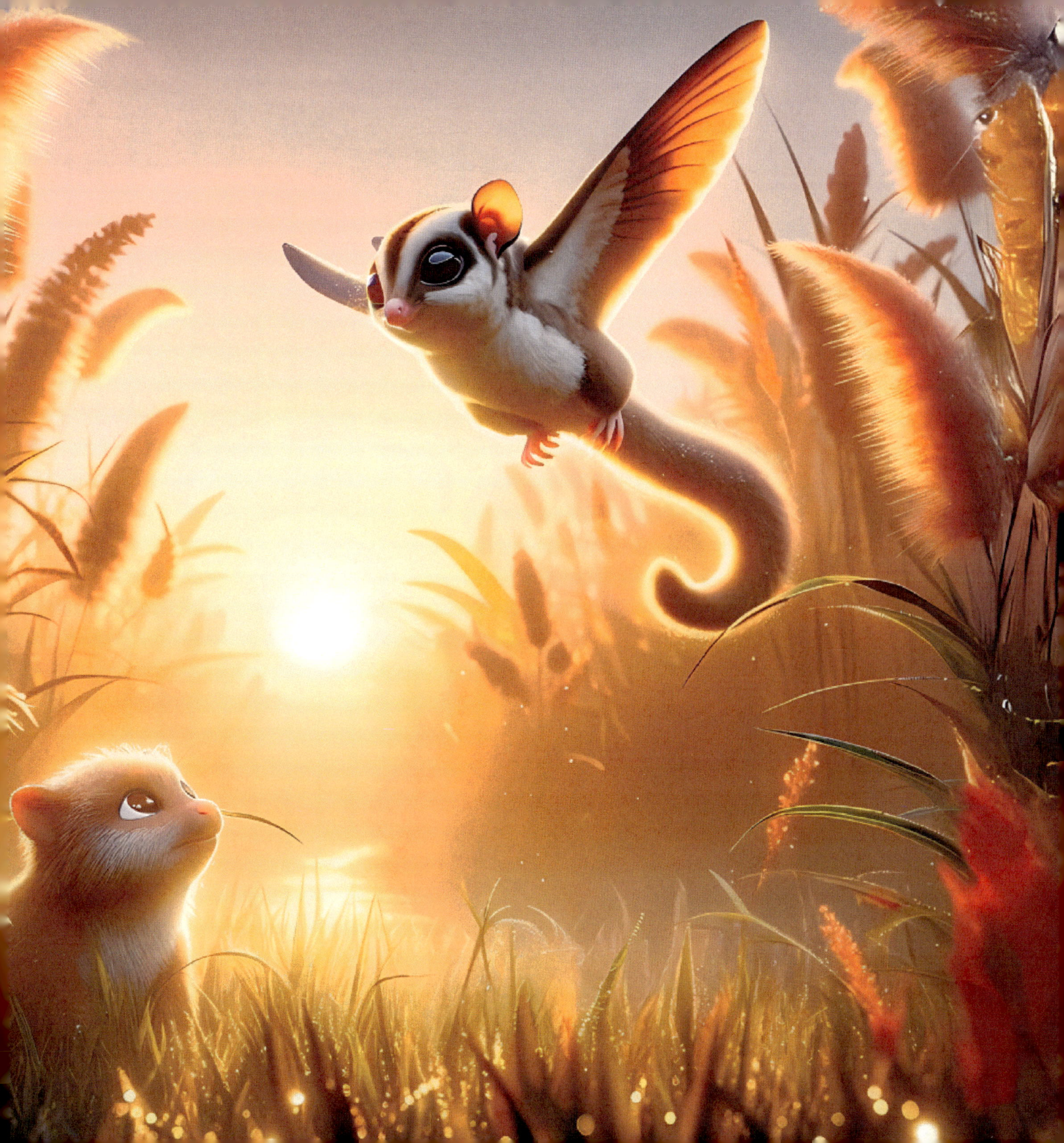

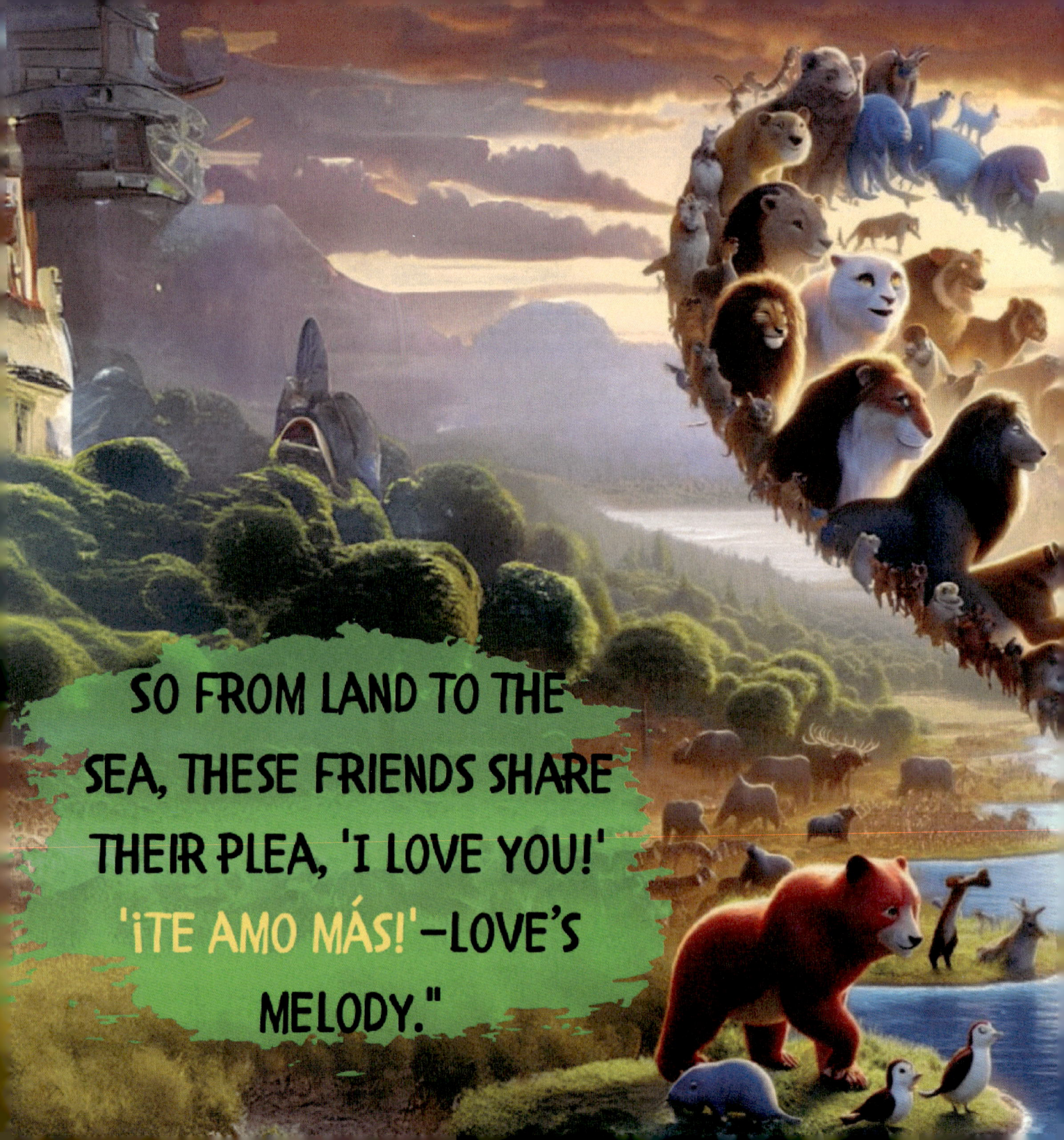

"So from land to the sea, these friends share their plea, 'I love you!' '¡Te amo más!'—love's melody."